Get it, Gus!

Written by Tina Pietron

Collins

Gus is a dog.

Gus is a pet.

Get it!

Gus

duck

4

Get the duck, Gus!

5

Tug at it, Gus!

Gus tugs at it.

Dip in it, Gus!

Gus dips in it.

Gus is in the mud.

No, Gus! Get up.

11

Gus sits in the sun.

I pat Gus.

pat

After reading

Letters and Sounds: Phase 2

Word count: 50

Focus phonemes: /g/ /c/ ck /e/ /u/ /o/

Common exception words: the, is, no, I

Curriculum links: Understanding the world

Early learning goals: Reading: read and understand simple sentences; use phonic knowledge to decode regular words and read them aloud accurately; read some irregular words

Developing fluency

- Your child may enjoy hearing you read the book.
- Take turns to read a page. Encourage your child to reread the whole sentence if they have hesitated over the exception words (**the**, **is**, **no**, **I**) or when blending any sounds.

Phonic practice

- On pages 2 and 3, ask your child to find the word with the /e/ sound, and to sound out and blend the word. (*p/e/t* – **pet**)
- On pages 4 and 5, ask your child to find a label with the /c/ sound, and to sound it out. (*d/u/ck*) Ask which two letters together make the /c/ sound. (*ck*)
- On page 6, ask your child to find a word that has the /u/ sound. (*Tug*) Next, ask them to find the word that has the /u/ sound on page 7. (*tugs*) Check they notice the extra "s".
- Look at the "I spy sounds" pages (14 and 15). Point to a puddle and say: I spy an /u/ in puddle. Challenge your child to point to and name different things they can see that begin with or contain the /u/ sound. (e.g. *umbrella, under, mud, mushrooms*). Point to the girl's envelope and say: I spy an /e/ in envelope. Encourage your child to point to other objects in the picture and listen out for the /e/ sound. (e.g. *elephant, eggs, nest, fence*)

Extending vocabulary

- Look through the first pages and point to the commands: page 4 **Get**; page 6 **Tug**; page 8 **Dip**. Look at the picture on pages 10 and 11 and ask your child: What would you ask Gus to do now? (e.g. *Get out, Get up, Come here, Run*)